Caring for Yourself while Caring for Others

Benedikte Exner

Copyright © Benedikte Exner 2014
This book is sold subject to the condition that it shall not, by way of trade or otherwise, be lent, resold, hired out, or otherwise circulated without the publisher's prior consent in any form of binding or cover other than that in which it is published and without a similar condition including this condition being imposed on the subsequent publisher.
The moral right of Benedikte Exner has been asserted.
ISBN: 1502973782
ISBN-13: 978-1502973788

I so agree that caring for myself is very important while caring for others – but how challenging it can be. I like the approach with the questions for the reader. It makes me think. I see this book as a tool. Often I return o the text to be reminded of it said and how I can use it.

- Susanne Stubager, nursing home nurse -

This book makes a lot of sense to me, and at the same time, it´s an eye opener - I must take care of myself in this profession. Lots of things to consider.

- Kirsten Jespersen, social worker with children -

This is really interesting to read and very precise. I feel so inspired to discuss this subject. In general I like the questions. It gives me an opportunity to reflect on my own situation.

- Jette Poulsen, social worker -

The subject is very relevant an useful for my own learning and self care. When I read the book as a superintendant, it can only please me, if an employee takes care of herself, and says a clear yes and no. Superintendants are often met with worn-out employees when it is far too late, and that is why this book is so important.

- Helle Winding, head nurse -

CONTENTS

Introduction 1

Chapter 1 4
Caring for Yourself - Caring for Others

Chapter 2 6
Breaks

Chapter 3 13
I Have To

Chapter 4 18
Who Listens to You?

Chapter 5 27
Conflicts

Chapter 6 40
Conscience

Chapter 7 48
Responsibility

Chapter 8 52
It Can't Be Right

Chapter 9 62
What is the worst that can happen?

Afterthought 72

Thank You 74

Background

For thirty years, I have worked as a professional carer. As a nurse I worked in hospitals, caring homes, in district nursing and as a nurse educator. For ten years I ran a home for mentally ill people. During that time I sought supervision, and I began more consciously to notice my own wants and needs, not only those of others. I became interested in how clients and working circumstances influence the personality of the professional caregiver, and how the caregiver's personality and actual state of health and mind influences his or her work.

I came to see how important it is that caregivers are aware of themselves and take care of themselves. During my ten years as a leader I trained for four years to be a psychotherapist. I continued as leader for some years and worked after that in alcohol treatment. Along with that I began supervising staff in social and health care and in private institutions.

As with most professional helpers - nurses, doctors, psychologists, teachers and private therapists - I am fortunately really good at caregiving. I and other professional caregivers can very quickly read the needs and the situation of the person we are helping. At the same time, most of us are not quite as good at feeling, accepting and acknowledging our own needs. It is very useful to be able to set aside our own needs in order to serve those who depend on us, or have bigger needs - whether it is children or challenged adults. But when this approach becomes automatic and unconscious, it is rather inexpedient. It leads to fatigue, stress, illness, lost joy in work, flight from the caring area, suppressed anger and internal conflicts between 'the good girls' (and boys). At the same time it veils our professional view. This does not serve anybody.

There has been a process in which 'the good girls' are not just good anymore. Demands on better work circumstances, wages, acknowledgment, supervision and education has been made very clear in many contexts, such as articles, books, the media, and at the negotiations between employers and employees. Yet, every day, thousands of caregivers - through our own actions - repress our own need for lunch, breaks, someone who will listen, appreciation and acknowledgment and respect for our professional skills and experiences. We try to fulfill unrealistic expectations from ourselves and others, and often we don't reflect as deeply on our own situation as we do on our clients, children, patients and relatives.

It is often said among us that we are good at caring for others, but not as good at caring for ourselves. I have heard - and said - this many times myself, with a cheerful self-irony, so it became a fact that wasn't even questioned at all.

The Purpose of the Book

In this book, I will focus on the caregivers' care and responsibility to themselves here and now. The book will bring about knowledge and awareness of this subject. The purpose is to increase the awareness in the individual caregiver, and working communities of caregivers. I call the book a book for reflection. My aim with the book is to make the caregiver reflect on how she or he is taking care of herself/himself.

My intention with this book is to contribute to your acceptance and acknowledgment of yourself, and to help you find more joy in your work. I have no doubt that a raised consciousness, and thereby a change in behavior of your care for yourself, will result in increasing the self-care of the people you are helping or working with. It is an ancient wisdom that others learn more from what we do than from what we say.

The Content and Composition of the Book

The book starts with a letter from me to the reader. I give a short resume of my own development, and what I am offering the reader.

My suggestion is that you read the Preface and *Caring for you While Caring for Others* as a start. The following chapters can be read independently and in random order. Every chapter looks at the professional caregiver's self-care from different perspectives. Every chapter contains knowledge, personal case stories and questions inviting reflection and consciousness in the reader, on how he or she treats himself/herself, and thereby others too.

The texts are without raised fingers. I do not want to dictate what is right or wrong, healthy or unhealthy. The latter you know all too well, or you will easily be able to gather relevant information. When it comes to right or wrong, it is absolutely not the intention of the book to increase your guilt or make you feel that there is even more you have to do. My aim is to invite to friendly awareness and caring for yourself, and consciousness about what works for you in your work. I use the words 'caregiver' and 'helper' randomly. These words are used in literature about people whose job it is to help others with personal needs and issues.

I have read a lot of literature within the areas of nursing, therapy, counseling, supervision and conflict management. I have come across very few books that deal with caregivers caring for themselves. So I have written one.

Introduction

Dear caregiver,

Ever since I started as a nursing student thirty years ago, I have been working with caregiving in a professional capacity. I have worked in hospitals, nursing homes, district nursing and as nurse educator. I have been manager of a home for the mentally ill and have worked with alcohol addiction. During the last four years I have been a supervisor for staff and managers within the caring professions.

Sixteen years ago I began to consider my own self-care, and to reflect on the links between our own self-care and our care for others.

I am writing to you, who are involved in caring for

others. You may be a nurse, teacher, care assistant, social worker, physiotherapist, occupational therapist, GP, psychologist, lecturer, independent practitioner or any other kind of caregiver. I know how important your work is. I am aware of the crucial difference you make to other people's lives, and also how much you gain from this yourself.

However, this work may come at a price. You may be wondering how you can direct some of this care towards yourself. Perhaps you feel that this is important for your own survival, or at least your health. You may feel the need to care more for yourself in order for you to continue being able to care for others - or to get better at it.

This is how it was - and is - for me. Several times in my life I have had to take a break and pay more attention to my self-care in order to feel alive and able to give to others. Because of this focus on myself I have become happier, freer and more honest with myself and others. I have come to the conclusion that the way I treat myself and how I treat others are one and the same issue. Through personal experience and the experience of others, it has become clear that the more we care for ourselves, the more we are able to care for others.

With this book, it is my hope to inspire you to care for yourself with compassion, and to take responsibility for your own health and wellbeing.

I feel like giving you lots of advice - instead, I have chosen to pose many questions. This is because my way of doing things may not be appropriate for you. I feel sure that you have wisdom enough to provide your own answers - also, that you have the ability to look up facts and figures if you need to. I may allow a few suggestions through the net, so use them if you like.

Best wishes - I hope you enjoy my book.

Chapter 1

Caring for Yourself - Caring for Others

There is no conflict between caring for myself and caring for others.

When I am being kind to someone else and I feel good about it, I feel happy.

When I treat someone else without kindness, I feel unhappy.

When I am kind to myself, I am able to give so much more to others.

When I receive help myself - even when I ask for help - it is easier for me to imagine what it is like for all those people I so want to help.

When I am harsh and unkind to myself or when I make sacrifices for others, feeling just a little irritated or unwilling, this will also be passed on to the ones I am trying to help and care for.

I have called my book *Caring for Yourself While Caring for Others* because I feel this aspect of caring needs to be highlighted. Fortunately, issues like care workers' salaries, working conditions, participation in the decision making process, and the need for supervision and further training, have all gained more attention recently.

It is equally important to attend to the way you care for yourself, however. It is your choice how you treat yourself, given the circumstances at the time. It becomes problematic when the misguided care of others leads to our own self-neglect, or when we become so angry and frustrated about the way other people neglect us that we deny ourselves any self-care. Problems arise when we believe that caring for ourselves is contradictory to caring for others - that they are separate issues.

During the safety announcement on airline flights, there is a section on oxygen masks. Here you are advised to always put your own oxygen mask on before helping others. How will you manage to think clearly and to act with efficiency when you need oxygen yourself?

Chapter 2

Breaks

Why is it sometimes so hard for caregivers to take breaks?

We know very well that body and brain need to recharge.

One explanation for why it is so hard might be that when we take a break, we risk discovering how we really are. This is an experience that many carers are not used to. Once I was convinced that I was feeling bad as a result of being weak or ungrateful, and if I felt well, I then felt guilty because so many others were unwell. I felt I needed to share my surplus energy instead of allowing myself to enjoy this feeling and maybe reflect on more appropriate ways to allow this feeling to benefit others. So, in a way, it was easier to be engaged in 'sensible' activity all the time, instead of being in touch with my true feelings.

Many helpers in the helping professions feel pressurized by working conditions. Sometimes there are so many tasks that it feels impossible to perform them in a professional, satisfactory and meaningful way. Many independent practitioners give themselves similar working conditions.

Carers might be thinking, 'If I take a break, my colleagues will suffer - or the patients, clients, children, residents, customers, users,' or, 'How can things carry on, if I take more breaks?'

Maybe you are familiar with this way of thinking. Do you recognize the more or less conscious conviction that everything will collapse, or you clients won't manage, if you don't push yourself relentlessly?

And is it true?

I think probably not. But you are the only one who knows.

Is it true that the world will collapse if you take those breaks that you need in order to feel well, in order to recharge, stay healthy and efficient, and retain job satisfaction? And if it really is true - what is it like to be working where there is no time for breaks? What is the atmosphere like for those you are caring for? If it all begins and ends with you, the world really is bound to collapse one day.

Perhaps you are afraid you will not be able to do your work well enough - maybe you fear losing your job or certain tasks, if you stop giving all the time. What is it like to work for someone who you imagine requires you to work relentlessly, without breaks?

Perhaps you worry that nothing will get done, if you take time for breaks.

I am not worried. I am getting used to feeling great joy working hard in a meaningful way both for me and others, as well as enjoying my breaks. My pleasure in taking breaks has not resulted in wishing that life can be put on hold. In fact, research suggests that a power nap or a chat increases productivity. So, why is it so hard for many caregivers to take breaks?

Some may be thinking, more or less consciously, 'I am worthless if I am not giving all the time. I need to be doing something sensible and productive (or look as if I am),' or, 'My identity is closely linked to what I can give or produce.'

Perhaps you are familiar with this belief set. Try asking yourself if this is true. If you still feel that this applies to you, then consider the people you are caring for, those who are not giving as much. Those whose whole life is like one

Caring for Yourself while Caring for Others

long break, whose lives are on hold. Do you feel that these people have an identity? Is it not the case that much of your work is about strengthening their sense of identity and helping them to feel their true worth?

In any case, it is actually impossible not to take breaks. I had a colleague once who was always late for appointments with his clients. He would often go from one appointment to the next without a break. Afterwards, he would admit to letting much of what had been said go in one ear and out the other. Our brain cuts out anyway when it wants a break. So why not take a break by paying full attention to ourselves, and then give our full attention to our work? When our bodies collapse due to stress, we get a break at last. Why wait that long?

As a child, I used to love seeing my mum lying in the sun with a book and a cup of tea. This looked so lovely and peaceful. Perhaps I also felt that her breaks meant that she would have more energy for me while I was growing up. It might be that those you are caring for will also enjoy the thought that you take breaks. They might be happy for you, and rejoice at the thought that you will feel well enough for longer.

And what if they were to discover that they could manage without you for a while... What a gift this would be for them, while you allow yourself a break.

If you recognize that these ideas about taking breaks apply to your life, and that you would like to change this pattern, I would suggest that you start by noticing when and how you take breaks. Notice also the times when you choose not to take a break, even if you feel you need one. Whether you have just started noticing the way you take breaks, or you have been aware of this for years, it is important to carry on from this point.

Try to become more aware of yourself from now on; maybe take time out to reflect on the nature of your breaks in the last month. Take note without judging - simply notice your choice of breaks and how these influence you and your work.

In the same way, notice how you might take 'secret' breaks; that is, times when we are not paying full attention to our work, nor taking actual breaks. These may be when we allow what is being said to 'go in one ear and out the other', or times when our brains 'cut out' and we stop paying attention to what is happening in the moment. This may also be when we spend time airing our frustrations without ensuring that these grievances can lead to real changes to whatever it is we are unhappy about.

Do not blame yourself if you take secret breaks; this is

something we all do now and then. If you take more secret breaks than you feel comfortable with, you can change this pattern once you have acknowledged it to yourself.

Once you are aware of your pattern of taking breaks and you have acknowledged to yourself how you really feel about it, the next step might be to set yourself more realistic goals for your pattern of breaks. Small steps will do to begin with; the important thing is to get started. Depending on the nature of your work, and your working hours, such goals could be:

• Next week I want to sit down to eat my lunch without interruptions, at least once.

• Tomorrow I am going to stop, breathe deeply and stretch, before moving on to the next task.

• During the next month I am going to set aside one morning per week to rest and recharge.

• From next month I will allow at least half an hour between appointments.

• At the next staff meeting I am going to introduce the subject of breaks. I want to tell the others how I feel about breaks, and I want to invite my colleagues to talk about the nature of their breaks and how they feel about this issue.

The more you practice taking breaks that are beneficial to you and to the way you work, the sooner it will become a good habit. Support and encouragement from others may be needed to facilitate this new habit of self-acknowledgement, setting yourself achievable goals and carrying them through into action.

Chapter 3

I Have To...

"I have to do that night shift - there is no one else who can do it."

"I have to pretend, even when what she is telling me makes me sad - because she is ill."

"I have to go to work, even though I haven't slept all night and I'm dizzy and unwell - otherwise my colleagues will have to cover. And what will my boss say? I have to go to work or I will appear weak."

"I have to answer the phone, even though I'm in the middle of something important."

"I have to listen to what he has to say because it sounds important. I admit he is rather drunk and may not remember anything in the morning - but if I dismiss him he might get angry and may not return."

"I have to show my new colleague the tasks in our department, even if my boss has said she will do it. It's embarrassing that it hasn't been done yet."

"I have to ignore that she is late and is not really up to the job. I have heard that things are difficult for her at home, and I would not want to add to her worries."

"I have to squeeze in this client tomorrow; this is a real crisis."

Do you recognize some of these beliefs, however conscious they may or may not be? There may well be many things you have to put up with in order to keep your job. On the other hand, perhaps there are fewer than you imagine.

Are you completely sure that you have to allow your meaningful, important task to be interrupted, just because someone else wants something from you? Are you completely sure that you have to sacrifice your own needs, job satisfaction and perhaps your health, in order not to lose your job?

It can be really challenging to ask yourself these questions. Personally, I have had to acknowledge that in order to remain true to myself and only be involved in tasks that I believed in, it felt impossible to remain in some workplaces, or to carry on with certain tasks.

The next question might be: Are you completely sure that you have to hang on to your job?

What is most important for you?

Consciously choosing your actions rather than doing what you feel you have to will strengthen your self-confidence and fill you with energy and vitality - even if you choose to do things you have done before. There is still a difference between choosing and 'having to' do something.

In the past, I really felt that I had to do so many things in order to maintain my self-image of this ever kind and helpful person who was always there for others. I had to ignore my own needs, dignity and self-worth in many different contexts. How liberating to discover that I did not have to retain this image of myself. Why on earth should I try to be so perfect when I am helping those who are less than perfect? I might even be helping them accept that they are not perfect. Does that seem honest?

It was wonderful to turn my attention to who I really am, rather than who I felt I ought to be. It was a huge relief to discover that I do not have to do things that feel unnatural to me or do not bring me joy. And it is particularly wonderful that I am not obliged to be less loving and helpful. On the contrary, whenever you are engaged in an activity because you feel you have to, particularly one that is not pleasurable or meaningful to you, you may discover a sense of unease in your body. Many people do not take such signals seriously, and we might even learn to ignore them completely.

See if you can notice what your body is signaling, particularly when you feel obliged to do a task: perhaps you get a headache, tension in your jaw or shoulders, knots in your stomach, tics in your eyelids or lips, or something else that you did not feel before, as soon as you begin a task that you feel you have to do, even if you do not want to right now.

Once you have identified a particular signal from your body, the next step might be to make a conscious decision whether to take it seriously. Consider carefully whether you really have to do whatever it is that you are about to do, and which feels so unappealing to you.

It might be going to work while running a temperature, accepting a task which you do not have time to do properly, listening to gossip, pretending all is well when you are sad - or whatever it is you usually feel obliged to get involved in.

It can be quite a struggle to change your beliefs about having to do certain tasks. Luckily it is possible to delay your reaction if you initially ignored your body's signals. It is perfectly possible to go home with a temperature after arriving at work, or to reconsider and turn down a task after all, or to go back and talk to the one who was gossiping or made you sad. The more you take your body's signals seriously in retrospect, the easier it will be to get into the habit of doing it in the moment. Support and encouragement from others may be needed to facilitate this new habit of self-acknowledgement, setting yourself achievable goals and carrying them through into action.

Chapter 4

Who Listens to You?

In your work, you are aware of the need to listen to those you are helping. This is really important; this attention to others boosts their self-confidence and gives them hope for improvement.

Clients, residents, patients, family, pupils, children and their parents may all share with you their worries and concerns. You experience many new aspects of life and gain satisfaction in helping others air their worries and grievances.

We are used to using the word 'listen' in the same way as the word 'hear'. The Chinese character for listening includes eyes, ears, heart as well as undivided attention. Whenever people in your care do not confide in you directly, you can experience their problems and pain through your other senses.

Working with people can affect us on many levels. Susanne Bang, social worker, psychotherapist and supervisor, writes about this in her book *Moved, Struck and Shaken*, a book about supervision.

Hopefully, being moved is an integral part of working with people. We feel happy when things are going well, and sad or angry when we witness hurt or sorrow. We are moved when we see people tackling life's challenges with dignity and creativity, and we feel touched by their expressions of gratitude. Naturally, how easily we are moved, how aware we are of this, and also to what extent we allow ourselves to be moved, varies considerably.

We can also feel struck or deeply affected when working with other people. Often this happens unconsciously to begin with. In the moment, we often do not notice the extent to which we feel affected. Sometimes, in cases that seem to be no different from so many others, we may react with irritation, confusion, too much or too little involvement, tiredness, sadness or resignation, or in other ways that differ from how we would normally react.

Too much involvement might mean ringing the client in your spare time, when this was not part of the deal. Or maybe wanting to be the only contact with the child and getting anxious when others take over. Or repeatedly cancelling other engagements in order to be available to a particular resident. Too little involvement might mean repeatedly forgetting appointments, pushing particular cases to the bottom of the pile, or being inattentive to certain clients, patients, children, parents or residents. If we are not conscious of what is happening and why, it may be because this particular case has hit one of our 'weak spots' or a 'blind spot'. This means that this case has reminded us of a psychological trauma or shock in our past which we have not yet managed to work through.

An example could be an illness that one of our nearest and dearest has suffered from. It could be the way a child is let down, reminding us of a similar experience in our own lives, or the lifestyle of someone that reminds us of what we ourselves long for. These are all conflicts that remind us of our own previous or current unresolved issues.

Caregivers can feel shaken when they witness something they had never imagined could happen, or when they experience physical abuse, threats or other ill treatment. It can be extremely frightening when our view of the world is extended or changed in this way.

Being moved, struck and shaken are all natural, human

reactions which most helpers and caregivers can expect to experience in their work. There is nothing strange or wrong about being affected by our work with other people. On the contrary, this gives us a better understanding of ourselves and we are better able to help others because we are more aware of our own 'weak spots'.

Problems arise when we do not acknowledge these reactions or take them seriously. In some workplaces it is considered weak or unprofessional, and therefore not acceptable, to react with compassion in our professional life. The subject is not mentioned and staff get used to hiding their emotional reactions from each other and eventually also from themselves.

However, which one of us is not weak and unprofessional once in a while? Is there anything wrong with that? It happens to all of us, so why not use it in a positive way? If we have someone to talk to, someone to be with no matter how we feel, someone who is mindful and interested in us, posing challenging and useful questions, then it becomes possible to regain our strength and professionalism.

There is strength and professionalism in recognizing our weakness and unprofessionalism! This way, it becomes easier to be empathic towards those we are trying to help, particularly when we receive care and attention ourselves. It is then that we acknowledge thoughts and feelings that have unconsciously affected our professional vision and responsiveness, and we regain our capacity for seeing and listening. This is part of our professional and personal development; we feel recharged and have more to give.

For health professionals working with severely traumatized individuals there is an added risk of suffering from secondary trauma. When experiences accumulate without being processed, our outlook can change so that we begin to look at the wider world with more worry, pessimism and negativity. It is also possible that we experience some of the symptoms that our traumatized patients and clients are suffering from, e.g. headache, palpitations, irritability, sleep deprivation, loss of appetite etc.

For this reason, it is appropriate, even essential, that we have various opportunities to process all the experiences we have at work.

It is important that colleagues and managers are available on a daily basis, so that we can offload thoughts and feelings and also exchange ideas. In acute, emotionally stressful situations, the provision of crisis counselling can be an advantage. With a view to longer-term professional development, it is appropriate to be in regular supervision with an external supervisor who is not involved in our workplace.

Obviously, it is important to feel safe and relaxed with those who are listening to us - both in our day-to-day routine and in scheduled meetings such as crisis help or supervision. This is particularly important in emotionally stressful situations when we often feel personally and subjectively affected, and therefore particularly vulnerable. In such cases, it is crucial to agree in clear terms about the best way to deal with the issues.

For the first many years of working, I had no idea that it was possible, through my workplace, to get help to process difficult and challenging experiences at work. Thinking back, I can see how much I missed having this opportunity without being fully aware of it.

I do remember a few episodes when the management were alert to this. This was in a ward for younger cancer patients. A couple of us nurses were very keen that a nineteen-year-old patient should speak to a psychologist because she was refusing to face up to the fact that she was going to die. Our ward sister made sure that we had an opportunity to speak to a psychologist about our own difficulty in accepting that she was going to die - and also about our difficulty in accepting that she did not want the emotional help we felt she needed.

When this young girl and another of 'my' patients died, my ward sister made sure we explored how this had affected us. At that time, I was not finding it easy to express how emotionally affected I was. Luckily, my ward sister was able to tell me how she thought I might be feeling. She also gave me a break from work with terminally ill patients for a while afterwards.

It was helpful when the ward sister was able to describe to me how I had become quieter and less cheerful than usual; I had not been conscious of this myself. Similarly, it was helpful when she told me how she thought I might be feeling, as I was in denial about the grief that had hit me. She told me how she knew what it was like to be so emotionally affected at work and this helped to validate my own feelings, so that I did not feel as if I had done anything wrong.

The ward sister's awareness and care of me contributed to a change of direction in my path towards burnout. While I took a break from my work with the terminally ill, I had space to process the way I had been so emotionally affected. I was able to see that some patients actually got better. I was otherwise starting to feel negative about my work, that, "It is no use - they are all going to die anyway."

Caring for Yourself while Caring for Others

It was only when I became the manager of a home for the mentally ill that I sought supervision for my work. My new place of work was in a private institution; my husband and I were going to manage this together, and we were going to be living there with our two young children. I was aware that this situation could become very complicated. I sought help in order to become a better leader professionally and also to be a better mum. It had been my choice that our place of work would become the home of our children. There were very good, sensible reasons for seeking help and advice.

I had not anticipated the way in which the supervisor was interested in how I was feeling. I was very surprised and cried for most of the first meeting - and on many other occasions afterwards. At the same time I felt hugely relieved, and I soon realized that my work would not suffer by looking after myself. On the contrary, in fact.

Who listens to you?

Who do you turn to when you are sad, angry, worried, scared, unsure or bubbling over with joy?

Are there colleagues or managers at work that you can talk to, when events at work have a particular effect on you or interfere with your professional judgment?

Is it possible to get emotional help in a crisis at work?

Is there a set-up at work where you can be the center of attention - where you can be heard by a trusted health professional, e.g. a supervisor or counsellor? Someone who can listen with interest and awareness, who can accept you as you are and pose important and thought-provoking questions?

Who is there for you in your private life? It may be that you have sometimes 'brought work home'. Is there anyone to share it with? In my experience, it is wonderful to have someone like that in your life. Family and friends are not involved in the same way that colleagues are. On the other hand, it can become a burden for family and friends to hear about the same problems at work again and again. They can listen and maybe help to gain a better insight into the problems in the short term. Longer term, it is important that our workplace can offer both professional and emotional help when needed.

Chapter 5

Conflicts

Conflicts are an unavoidable part of life in society and in the workplace. However, even though conflicts are so unavoidable, many of us believe that they should not exist at all. This belief makes it more difficult to deal with them.

Perhaps you are stuck in a conflict with a colleague, a manager, a client, a child, an adolescent, a parent, a patient or another important person?

I trained as a mediator with The Danish Centre for Conflict Resolution and for a number of years I have been trying to get better at dealing with conflicts in a more appropriate way, within myself as well as with others. My point of departure is that everyone deep down wants the best for themselves and others. Often, this is not how it looks once a dispute has taken hold. When communication has broken down, has got stuck or becomes offensive and blaming, it is hard to hang on to this belief. When basic rights and needs are being violated, or we are not being heard or acknowledged, when we are told off, blamed or harassed in other ways, it can be really hard to believe that the relationship can be restored.

Luckily, matters can always be improved, at least for yourself, if you really want it. You have no control over the other party, no matter how much you fight for that control. However, your way of expressing yourself can have a significant impact on yourself and the other - and thereby have an impact on the conflict itself.

Fundamentally, there are three ways to respond to a conflict: to avoid, to fight and to face the conflict head-on. All of these can be used appropriately as long they are chosen consciously.

It might be wise to avoid a conflict if the other party is much stronger and not inclined to dialogue, or if the matter is not important to you. Sometimes fighting might be the best choice. If you really feel very strongly about a certain case, and there is no immediate possibility for dialogue, taking the case to court or practicing civil disobedience might give you more peace of mind and a clearer conscience. Fighting a case with physical or verbal abuse will only result in making matters worse. This approach is never advisable, unless you really want to keep the dispute going without a resolution.

I have noticed a tendency to avoid conflicts in the health professions. They do not go away with this approach, but live on in the form of gossip, becoming a drain on energy levels and job satisfaction. Do you recognize this observation? Do you know what it is like to be in dispute with someone without being able to talk it through with them? Do you know what it is like to be talking to everyone else about this dispute?

Personally, I have been in this situation many times. I have often found myself seething with anger without knowing how to handle a dispute. An example is when I was working as a district nurse in a small town. It was my weekend off and I had gone to the local street market. Suddenly I felt a tap on the shoulder from a colleague. It was her shift and she needed someone to do the night shift that same evening. She had gone to the market as she could not get hold of any of the other nurses over the phone. We were having visitors and I had been looking forward to the weekend. I was well aware that I did not feel like going to work at all. Nevertheless, it never occurred to me to say no or to tell the nurse in question how it felt to be approached like this on my day off. Instead, I spent the evening complaining about her insensitive approach, all the while condoning her method by turning up for the night shift that evening.

We can wonder whether my headache and resulting sick-day during the following week was due to these thoughts about what had happened. I remember clearly how I regaled my colleagues with my sense of injustice at being approached in this way, and how it had spoilt my weekend.

These days I know that I could have politely declined without catastrophic consequences. And if my thoughts about what had happened had continued to sour relations between me and the other nurse, I know that I could have talked to her about it. And she could have talked to me if she could not accept my answer.

In this chapter I want to focus on ways to meet a conflict openly, with the intention of resolving it and maintaining the relationship with the other party. The following guidelines have been shown to have a calming effect on situations of conflict, allowing contact to be maintained:

- Acknowledge your thoughts, feelings and wishes
- Express them clearly
- Be interested in the thoughts, feelings and wishes of the other party
- Do not blame or attack. This blocks any further contact and causes a defensive stance - or in the worst cases a counter attack.
- Do not allow the other party's attacks and accusations to get under your skin. This is not beneficial to him or her, either.
- Consider whether some of what you are being accused of is actually true. Is there anything you would like to change about your behavior?

Often, we are under the impression that everything will get a lot worse if we do things differently from the way we are used to. After all, we feel safe with what we are familiar with, even if the matter is uncomfortable, e.g. a conflict which has become stuck, or maintaining the same inappropriate approach to conflict resolution.

We might feel that if we start to listen with understanding, we might be defeated or lose face. We might also expect the other party to become even angrier if we set clear boundaries for what we are prepared to do. In most cases, none of these fears are justified. Deep down, most people have the same basic needs: sustaining life, being loved, validated and respected, and achieving a balance between security, freedom and challenges.

Nevertheless, the ways in which we want these needs to be met differs enormously from person to person. This fact is the cause of many misunderstandings. People often assume unconsciously that others feel the same way as themselves: "There must be something wrong with one of us as we do not understand each other!"

But when we listen openly and are true to our own feelings, thoughts and needs, a change occurs. As soon as we recognize one of our own basic needs in the other, we feel more respectful of them. And as soon as we feel listened to and respected, we start to relax and feel like opening up and listening ourselves.

In those cases, when both parties feel understood by each other, it is usually quite easy to negotiate a practical solution acceptable to both. I have often observed this happening almost automatically.

As an example, two of my supervisees, working together as part of a multidisciplinary team, could not agree on the best approach in the case of a withdrawn, unmotivated patient in a psychiatric care home. It seemed as if both colleagues were more intent on winning the argument than helping the patient. When one of them revealed how important it was for her to be taken seriously as a professional, as well as being able to adopt the professional approach most meaningful to her, the other recognized these needs within herself. They now both saw how the patient could benefit equally from both viewpoints. They agreed, without further ado, to meet up two days later to discuss the next course of action. Similarly, both were motivated to learn more about the other's professional viewpoint. And neither of them felt threatened professionally any longer.

On the other hand, it is important that you admit to yourself if, right at this minute, you do not feel like listening openly, with interest, and that you give yourself permission to feel like this. Deep down you want to listen and express an opinion, but sometimes this wish is buried deep down under many layers of disappointment, confusion and strong emotions or maybe even exhaustion, numbness or hopelessness.

Sometimes the best and most honest approach might be to take a break in communications. It is much more beneficial to the relationship to be honest about the lack of any real communication, than pretending it is there.

During these breaks in the talks, it is useful to talk to yourself - or someone not involved in the conflict - about how you are feeling, and what kind of relationship you want with the other party. This short list - inspired by Marshall Rosenberg's *Nonviolent Communication* - could be helpful:

- Facts: What has happened?
- Thoughts and feelings: what is the conflict doing to me?
- Needs: What do I want?
- Request: How can I get what I want?

It is really important to stick to the facts. For example, it will intensify the conflict if you say, "You are always late." However, the statement, "Three times last week you were more than ten minutes late," is much more to the point.

Similarly, it will intensify the conflict to say, "You don't care about me at all." It is more to the point to say, "You are at the door, hand on the door handle, not looking at me; this makes me feel as if you don't care about me and that makes me sad."

The latter way of putting it validates your own feelings

without blaming the other. You take responsibility for your own thoughts and feelings. The other party does not need to become defensive, making it easier to open up and listen to you.

When expressing a need or a wish, it helps to put it in general terms as this makes it easier for the other party to understand. For example: "It is important to me that my time is respected." The other party has similar needs, although this need might be met in other ways than always being punctual.

Once your needs are clear to yourself, it becomes much easier to formulate a request clearly.

"I would like us to make plans together that are realistically achievable for you. And I would like you to tell me if you are going to be more than five minutes late."

Other examples could be:

(Caregiver to patient/client/resident/youth/relative)

- Facts: you have just called me a bitch and you have said that my help is worse than nothing.

- Thoughts and feelings: this makes me very sad (and/or angry) as I have invested a lot of care and attention to your case.

- Needs: I really want to help you, and it is important to me that we can work together.

- Request: please tell me what you expect from me. I would like to find out what I may have said or done that is worse than nothing to you. Please try not to shout at me as this makes me want to help you less.

(Colleague to colleague, working under the same manager)

- Facts: you are telling me that you are sick of our poor management. You have said this several times in the last weeks.

- Thoughts and feelings: I know what you mean, and I recognize much of what you are telling me. At the same time, I am getting tired and irritated, listening to you.

- Needs: I would very much like to maintain our professional relationship. Similarly, I would really like to see some changes at work.

- Request: Why don't we sit down together and try to verbalize how we both feel in the current situation? Maybe write down what we would like the management to address?

Caring for Yourself while Caring for Others

(Colleague to manager)

• Facts: I now have 60 cases, 12 of which are really complex. According to current guidelines, we should only be dealing with a caseload of 40.

• Thoughts and feelings: I am exhausted and feel guilty that I can't manage everything. I worry about not being able to cope in the long run. I get headaches a couple of times a week and I do not sleep as well as I used to. Also, it makes me a bit nervous talking about this, and I wonder if I will get fired if I can't take the pressure.

• Needs: I would really like to keep my job; I like my job and want to do it well. I need to be able to stick to what is my responsibility and allocated tasks.

• Request: I would like to know what you think about what I just said, and also what you expect of me in this situation. If you can't reduce my caseload, will you help me find a way to prioritize?

(Manager to care worker)

• Facts: your group colleagues are concerned about you. In the last two weeks you have forgotten at least three meetings. You often seem irritable, giving curt, angry responses with no eye contact. Many of us have smelt alcohol on your breath at least once this week.

- Thoughts and feelings: I am sorry to see you like this. I know that you are normally committed and engaged in your work and that you enjoy it. I am not quite sure about your contribution at the moment.

- Needs: your colleagues and I would like to work with you in the team. It is important to me that the department runs smoothly and that you all, together and individually, enjoy your work and carry out all your tasks.

- Request: first of all, I would like know how you feel about what I have just said.

These examples are presented schematically, and they may come across as artificial if used verbatim. However, to prepare for a difficult conversation, it can be useful to follow this structure.

On top of the four elements in this approach, there is a fifth: My contribution - how can I contribute? This is as important as the other four questions. Having thought this through beforehand, and after the other party has told you how they feel, it is important to consider their requests carefully and honestly. By that I mean truly wanting to contribute whatever it is you are suggesting. This is so that you avoid making sacrifices to achieve a temporary truce.

When two conflicting parties want to achieve a resolution while acknowledging that this is beyond their capabilities, it might be possible to seek the help of a mediator. The aim is to allow this neutral third party to lead the process so that the parties can express themselves freely, listen to each other, offer suggestions, negotiate and make deals without offending the other. The mediator does not take sides in the conflict and has no say in its resolution. The conflict is between the two parties - and so is the resolution.

Conflicts are part of life and none of us can avoid them. It is the way we choose to handle conflicts that is the issue. The good thing about conflicts is that they can make the implicated parties grow and develop, as well as lead to better relations and increased intimacy.

Good luck with yours.

Chapter 6

Conscience

As you know, our conscience can be clear or guilty. Let us look at the guilty conscience first. In my experience this is flourishing among professional caregivers. They are controlled by an urge to avoid having a guilty conscience.

What does having a guilty conscience actually mean?

- I ought to… but I don't do it.
- I mustn't do…whatever it is I'm doing.
- I shouldn't have done…whatever it is that I did do.
- I should have done….whatever it was I didn't do.

A guilty conscience always feels uncomfortable - simply because you are doing one thing while thinking you should be doing something else. In this way, you are doing something wrong in your own eyes. Notice that this exactly what characterizes the statements above: my actions are in conflict with what I feel I should be doing instead.

A guilty conscience indicates that there is a discrepancy between my actions and my intensions. It doesn't tell me what is right or wrong. Thus, a guilty conscience is not a healthy warning that I am about to do something wrong. When I have a guilty conscience, or in other words, when I am doing something I have learnt or I believe I should not do, thoughts and questions go round and round in my mind. I am weighed down by guilt and I feel drained of energy. This is really uncomfortable. I do what I do - and at the same time it feels wrong.

When I do something that goes against my own convictions, I am in touch with different feelings. I might feel sad, angry or restless - this is different from having a guilty conscience. This is equally uncomfortable because here, thoughts and actions are also in conflict - only the other way round. In this case, I am kidding myself that I am doing something right while my body and my feelings are protesting. This is uncomfortable - but less deadening than having a guilty conscience. In this case, I am in touch with my own feelings and whatever it is that would ease my conscience.

Yet, it is never this simple, of course. When we experience having a guilty conscience with lots of confusing thoughts, we also have uncomfortable feelings. By separating a guilty conscience from actions that go against our own convictions, I want you to explore if your actions go against your own values or those of others when you feel uncomfortable about what you are doing. There is a difference and with the right awareness we can learn to separate the two.

How can a guilty conscience be of use to me?

My guilty conscience tells me exactly what I believe is expected of me. This realization can be very interesting. What expectations are ruling my life? Whose rules do I live under? Whose needs are more important to me? What do I believe that other people expect of me? What expectations do I have of myself? How realistic are they?

When I am hungry and take a break to eat, I may feel guilty. My guilty conscience is caused by my belief that others - colleagues, patients, children, parents, clients, managers - all think I should be working even when I am hungry.

When I am hungry and carry on working instead of stopping to eat, I may do that in order to avoid the guilty feelings. I allow myself to be ruled by my fear of guilt. I avoid the guilt - instead, I become angry and resentful with the person whose needs I believe I am providing for (this often happens unconsciously, or in small glimpses that are quickly denied).

When I am hungry and I do not take a break to eat, I might feel guilty anyway. In this case I might be thinking of Health and Safety regulations, my friend or the health guru in the newspaper, or whoever thinks that I should eat when I am hungry.

When I am hungry and I consciously choose to eat, I am taking myself and my job seriously. I am looking after myself and I work more efficiently when I am not hungry. I have a clear conscience.

When I am hungry and I consciously choose to finish a particular piece of work before I eat, and when I kindly tell myself why I feel it is better to keep working, while reminding myself when I can be allowed to eat, I have a clear conscience.

How can this be? Well, my thoughts are now in tune with my actions. I am doing what I feel to be right, while taking the consequences of my decision; this means my conscience is clear. This might feel complicated, but I am at least at peace with myself; it is difficult to be in conflict with this 'self', which is always there for me to relate to.

Do you know what it is like to have a guilty conscience?

Have you ever felt controlled by unclear expectations?

Are you familiar with the joy of having a clear conscience?

As mentioned earlier, a guilty conscience can control so many actions. However, in today's society there is a tendency towards remarks like, 'You don't need to feel guilty about that.' This can lead me to feel guilty about feeling guilty when it is unnecessary, so all of a sudden I have two problems instead of one.

I am more truly at peace with myself when I explore my guilty conscience, rather than trying to make it go away.

We will all have a guilty conscience now and then. That's just how it is. Why not use it in a creative way rather than fighting it? Every time I have a guilty conscience, I have an opportunity to explore the expectations I have of myself. Are they too great? Are they really my own expectations or have I taken on those of others? Is there anything I would have done differently? What can I learn from this experience?

For many years I was controlled by my guilty conscience. In a way, this worked really well. I did not feel guilty as long as no one was unhappy with what I was doing. I was not interested in consciously exploring what I really wanted deep down. I was more interested in - and rather good at - interpreting what other people wanted from me. Often I was unhappy without being able to understand why. I thought I was doing so well, felt appreciated by most people and received much praise.

I became aware that the problem arose when I felt that my surroundings had different - even contradictory - expectations of me. It was impossible to be in more than one place at a time. It was really difficult to try and decide whose needs were greatest. Sometimes, when I had not listened to my own needs, I was aware of feeling angry and sad. I might become furious with a poor patient because I always allowed his needs to come first - or at least what I took to be his needs. Of course, I did not openly show this anger. Instead I gained some release by gossiping with colleagues about his unreasonable demands. Looking back now, I can forgive myself - I did not know what else to do.

There was nothing wrong with wanting to have my own needs met while helping others. The problem was that I did not take responsibility for prioritizing there and then. I can't change my actions from that time. I can learn from them. I can become better at accepting and living with the fact that I am fallible. I can become better at forgiving myself.

My personal and professional lives have become enriched and more manageable since I started listening to my clear conscience, rather than trying to avoid my guilty conscience.

If you would like to feel less controlled by your guilty conscience, you could start by noticing your motivation when you are really engaged in a task. I often ask myself this question: 'Am I doing this in order to achieve something positive or in order to avoid trouble?' Depending on your area of work, you could ask yourself:

- "Did I allow this patient or child to decide because it gives me pleasure and because there are valid, professional reasons for this? Or did I do it in order to avoid upsetting the patient, with the risk of making myself feel guilty?"

- "Did I break off this conversation with a client, child or relative because I did what was needed and felt happy with the outcome? Or did I do it in order not to feel guilty about spending too much time on this, while my colleagues were busy with so many other tasks?"

If you have noticed that you often feel controlled by your guilty conscience, you can set yourself some goals for change:

- "At least on two occasions tomorrow I want to consciously choose to channel my energies into achieving something for myself rather than trying to avoid feeling guilty."
- "The next time I become aware of feeling guilty, I want to turn my attention towards what I can best achieve in this situation and let this govern my actions."

Paradoxically, you will perhaps discover that the less you fight your guilty conscience, the less it will govern you. Support and encouragement from others may be needed during this process of self-acknowledgment, setting yourself achievable goals and carrying them through into action.

Chapter 7

Responsibility

Being responsible - able to respond.

I choose my own responses - consciously or not. I am responsible for what I say or do in relation to patients, relatives, residents, children, parents, colleagues, managers and employees - no matter what they are doing. The fact is that I can choose my own words and actions. I cannot choose what others do or say.

It is my responsibility to choose if I go to work today. I am responsible for what I contribute at work, once I have chosen to turn up. I am responsible for what I ask of myself and for whoever I allow to manipulate me. Perhaps you are familiar with the Serenity Prayer, used by Alcoholics Anonymous (AA) and attributed to Reinhold Niebuhr:

God grant me the serenity to accept the things I cannot change, the courage to change the things I can, and wisdom to know the difference.

The Serenity Prayer is very useful. It truly requires serenity to allow others to make choices that I find it difficult to understand. It takes courage to realize how much power I have over my own life and to begin to change what I can. Wisdom is essential in order to be able to differentiate which doors to go through, so that I choose the ones I can open rather than continuing to knock on those that are locked to me.

Many of us spend a lot of time feeling guilty about things that we cannot control - at the same time turning a blind eye to what we can truly change. It is very easy for us to focus on what others should be responsible for. We can think and talk for hours about our useless managers or employees. I have done both for years.

However, we cannot change our managers and employees. On the other hand, we can change our response to them. This is what determines what our responsibility is.

When we respond with honesty to what we experience, we often find that the situation changes - that the other person changes. Deep down, no one really wants to make us sad, angry or dissatisfied. First and foremost everyone wants to do a good job.

Once I had become aware of the need to care for myself, I discovered how much responsibility I was taking for others. I became aware how much I was struggling to try and make sure others had their needs met. I began to see myself as 'super responsible'.

I spoke to other helpers who had started to notice something similar in their own lives. We agreed that it was hard work and pretty unproductive to feel 'super responsible'. We had to make changes. Even so, it felt more acceptable to be 'super responsible' than 'super irresponsible'. In our eyes, the 'super irresponsible' did not care about us or how we were feeling.

Later I had to acknowledge that the term 'super responsible' is not as meaningful to me any longer. It turns out that when I feel 'super responsible' for others, I am 'super irresponsible' for myself.

Nowadays I know that when I take responsibility for myself here and now, I leave others to take responsibility for themselves - this does not mean that I cannot offer

Caring for Yourself while Caring for Others

them joy and intimacy. On the contrary.

How do you respond when your back is telling you that it is tired or hurting?

How do you take responsibility for your back? (Not to respond is also a response)

How do you respond when your anger indicates that your values are being challenged? How do you take responsibility for your anger?

How do you respond to:

- Your bad back?
- Your aching head?
- Your insecurity and fear?
- Your irritation with conditions at work?
- Your anger at unfair treatment?
- Your joy at doing what you are good at?
- Your joy at doing what you feel like doing?
- Your longing for…?
- Your wish for…?

Chapter 8

It Can't Be Right…

When I supervise professional caregivers and helpers, I often hear spontaneous remarks like, "That can't be right," or, "That's out of order," or, "I just don't believe it." These remarks are said in a context where everyone agrees that whatever it is that 'can't be right' has actually happened. For example:

"My manager asked me to do an extra weekend shift two days after I had told him how much I need a rest. I don't believe it."

"We were really busy, but my colleague walked straight past us

Caring for Yourself while Caring for Others

and sat down with a cup of coffee. That really is out of order."

"He was smelling of alcohol, but said he had not been drinking since he was here last. He can't lie to my face like this."

"I asked my manager a really important question, but she didn't respond to it. That just can't be right."

"It can't be right that one of my colleagues has not addressed the fact that the child she is looking after has played truant from school. It can't be right that the first I hear of this is from a puzzled teacher. In addition, it has been several weeks since the teacher brought this to her attention."

"For the third time in two weeks, this child has forgotten his packed lunch - and he keeps forgetting his slippers. You can't treat your own child in this way."

"I have worked so hard with this client concerning this particular problem, but he has not changed one bit. That can't be right."

Are you familiar with thinking and talking like this in similar situations? Perhaps you do not feel that there is anything wrong with thinking like this. In some ways, there really is nothing wrong with it as we all do it to a greater or lesser degree. We often say such remarks out loud, and we often hear others speak in this way. Nevertheless, it is interesting to look at such remarks in more detail. We are often frustrated and exhausted when we think and talk in this way.

In each of the examples above, our thoughts are in conflict with what is actually happening in front of our eyes. Fighting against reality is always uncomfortable because this battle is lost from the start. But that does not mean we cannot do anything about our frustration with reality!

I am fascinated by the extent to which we can deny the facts - even without being aware of it. When I point out to my supervisee that he or she has made such a remark, they are usually unaware of this themselves. I was unaware myself during all those years when I did not feel I could/dared/wanted to believe that people really do behave in this way.

Where does this tendency to deny the facts comes from, I wonder?

Johan Cullberg, a Swedish psychiatrist, explains that we do it in order to defend against a reality that cannot be endured at present. In an emergency, it can be useful to deny an event and to allow reality to come into consciousness in 'bite-sized chunks'. When we have no idea what to do in new situations, we can feel safer by denying reality until we are ready to face up to the actual situation e.g. because of seeking help with it.

Caring for Yourself while Caring for Others

However, by automatically denying larger or smaller parts of our everyday lives, we are closing ourselves off to parts of ourselves and our surroundings. In addition, we are sabotaging ourselves unintentionally; by refusing to face up to reality, it becomes impossible for us to change it. By denying the reality, we are actually preventing ourselves from getting what we want.

For a moment, we kid ourselves that this cannot be right. It is like wetting your pants when it is really cold - it feels warm for a short while, but even colder afterwards. We warm ourselves by the thought that this cannot be right, and then we feel cold afterwards. And we feel even colder because we allow whatever it is that we do not like to pass without complaint (if not without comment). In this way it looks as if we agree with what has happened - and naturally, this feels very frustrating for us.

We are only able to change the things that we accept. By this I do not mean 'not mind' or 'agree to'. What I mean is accepting what has happened as reality. If I want to change a situation which is unacceptable to me, I will need to experience the pain of accepting that the situation actually is - or was - very real.

My manager did actually ask me to do a weekend shift at a time that was inconvenient for me - either he had overheard, forgotten or ignored what I told him two days ago.

My colleague did not help me when I was busy. She sat down with a cup of coffee.

The alcoholic client, who I really want to help, is actually lying to my face.

My manager did not respond to my question, even if it was really important to me.

This employee has not responded to important information about the child she is responsible for.

The parents of this child are not making sure that he brings a packed lunch and slippers every day.

This client has not changed one bit in relation to this particular problem, even after we have worked on it for so long.

That is how it is. What is my job now? What would I like to achieve or contribute? What do I want to do now?

By facing up to reality, just the way it is, we are doing the opposite of wetting our pants in order to feel warm. We accept a temporary feeling of discomfort, thus enabling us to choose how to respond in order to change the situation or dealing with our frustration about it. In this way we can find a more durable happiness.

Naturally, we cannot change everything that we accept

as reality. But this way, we can consciously let go of what cannot be changed. Instead, we can focus on all those situations we do have some control over. We can control our own actions in any given situation. We choose our own responses to those who do the things that, initially, we cannot believe are right.

It is important to accept reality, and equally important to accept our own reaction to our surroundings. Are you familiar with thoughts like, 'It can't be right that I became so upset,' or, 'I really can't allow myself to get so angry about such a small matter,' or, 'It just can't be right that I got so disappointed'?

Yes, it really can be right. You do actually get so upset, angry, disappointed etc. By accepting that fact, and by giving yourself, or allowing others to give you, space to feel this way, you will be able to choose your course of action more easily.

I know very well that it is not always possible to see the choices we have in the situations we would normally be in denial about. I am well aware that it can be difficult to take action in cases where your manager does not respond to your questions or requests. In particular, when the question is important to you, and the answer has significance for you and your work. I have experienced this myself many times -

both as co-worker, manager, colleague and supervisor.

It can feel really challenging to say to your boss, "Right now you are not answering my question." However, I can promise you that by asking in this way, the situation is more likely to change than if you are still saying to yourself or your colleagues, "She didn't even answer my question. That can't be right!"

If you repeatedly allow your manager to get away with avoiding answering your questions, she may well carry on in this way whenever she is struggling to respond. This will hardly feel very satisfying for her, either. However, this can be a way for her to avoid uncomfortable situations. This will lead to more unhappiness and you will slowly lose respect for her and - less consciously - yourself. This will not help you to respect your clients, colleagues, employees, patients, children, parents or residents - cf. the oxygen mask on the plane.

However, by accepting that right at this minute your manager is not answering your question, and by accepting your own reaction to this, you will have a range of possible actions to take. In such situations, our options will generally fall into three categories: Accept, change or leave.

In workplace situations, these options might be expressed in the following three ways:

Caring for Yourself while Caring for Others

- Accept certain negative aspects in your job and channel your energy into the positives.

- Change the situation - or comment on what is happening, while maybe sharing how it makes you feel, with the aim of changing the situation.

- Leave the meeting (or any other situation) for a short time while you collect your thoughts. You might even leave the workplace completely.

With regard to the example when your manager does not respond to you, your options might be:

1a. You have time to reflect, making you realize that although your manager will usually always respond very clearly, you asked her at a time when she was very busy. This makes it easier to accept that she did not respond in this case.

1b. You have time to reflect, sharing with a colleague how irritated you feel. You realize that it is typical of the manager to act in this way. You become aware that an unclear response has the positive effect of allowing you to act in your own way. You have wonderful colleagues and you can usually do your job satisfactorily. These positives are so important to you that you can accept the way in which the manager is not always as clear as you would like.

2. After some reflection, you realize how important it is for you to get a response. You allow space for your feelings and so you calmly say to your boss, "I asked you if... and you replied that... Please will you answer my question?"

3a. You feel tearful and you are unable to utter a single mature, professional or sensible word. You start to cough and you leave the room. In this breathing space, you reflect on what you need and what your next step might be. This could be 1a, 1b, 2, 3b or something completely different; this will only become apparent when you have calmed down enough to think clearly.

3b. You are reminded of the many times in the past when you did not receive an answer. You remember the many times you have directly asked for a reply without getting it. You realize that you need clear responses in order to be able to do your work satisfactorily. You realize that your expectations of the management are not being met in this workplace and you decide to find another job.

These procedures apply to the other examples (often, one of the three options will seem unacceptable, leaving you with 'only' two). For example, there is the situation

Caring for Yourself while Caring for Others

where you are really busy while a colleague walks straight past you on her way to her coffee break. If you cling on to the belief that this cannot be right, you risk being eaten up by rage while outwardly feeling paralyzed. This can give the impression that you are not struggling with this situation. However, if you accept the reality of the situation, you can choose to accept, change or leave.

You accept the fact that you are busy because you know what time you will be finished. In this way, you can leave your colleague's decisions to her. It might be that she has been even busier than you.

You ask your colleague to help you finish the job. She may not realize how hard you have been working without a break.

You leave the task in hand and join your colleague for coffee. You were reminded of your own need for a break when you saw her walk past.

It can't be right that it is that simple (not easy, but simple) - or can it?

Chapter 9

What is the worst that can happen?

If you have read as far as this, or even if you have started with this chapter, you are probably willing to start taking better care of yourself and to continue developing this skill. It can be interesting to explore what is preventing us from doing what we really want to do and refusing to do whatever makes us feel uncomfortable. It is often unclear to many of us what we truly want; we are held back by our equally unclear fears about what might happen if we really did follow our own needs, interests and intuitions.

The question, "What is the worst that can happen?" can be a useful tool in exploring these unconscious blocks.

Unless we explore our unconscious fears, we will not be able to identify the true nature of what is at stake. Equally, we will not be able to decide whether our fears about a new course of action are more or less realistic. We may not even be aware that we are fearful. Thoughts like, 'Wow, how am I going to manage this?' or, 'I'm sure this patient is lying, but I really can't say anything,' or, 'Why didn't I say what I really meant?' are all evidence that we are ignoring the urge to seek help, or to express our doubts or opinions.

Why on earth would you ignore common sense? Because, unconsciously, we fear the consequences of acting on it.

So, in order to be able to ask, "What is the worst that can happen?" we will have to become aware of our fear - or at least our doubts and concerns.

Perhaps you are familiar with the examples - or similar - below:

- "I am afraid to ask for help with this task."
- "I am afraid to admit that I do not trust this patient."
- "I am afraid to openly disagree with the management."
- "I am afraid to tell my colleague that I am worried about her."

- "I am afraid to talk to this employee about the tasks she is not performing well enough."

- "I am afraid to confront these parents with my thoughts about negligence."

- "I am afraid to say no to more night shifts."

- "I am afraid to tell this employee that I doubt her ability to do her work."

Are you familiar with some of these thoughts - or is there another situation when you were afraid to follow your immediate impulse? Our fears can take many different shapes, and the chances of them being realized are more or less probable in real life. However, by asking the question, "What is the worst that can happen?" we will inevitably get closer to reality rather than phantasy.

In the next section I have posed some questions related to the statements above. I have suggested a reply, followed by some additional, probing questions.

- What is the worst that can happen if you were to ask for help with this task? *If I ask for help, my colleagues will think I am stupid/weak/unfit for this task.*

- What would you think if a colleague asked you for

help? Do you really think that all your colleagues will think you are stupid/weak/unfit? What is the worst that can happen if one or two think like that? How does it feel not to ask for the help you need?

- What is the worst that can happen when you admit that you do not trust your patient? *If I admit to not trusting my patient/client, she will never confide in me again.*

- Are you quite sure that your patient will never confide in you if you admit to not trusting her? Is it possible that your honesty would increase her trust in you? What is the worst that can happen if she stops confiding in you? How does it feel when you pretend to believe what she is saying when you really do not believe her?

- What is the worst that can happen when you openly disagree with the management? *If I openly disagree with my managers, they will become frustrated with me.*

How realistic is it that your managers will become frustrated if you express your disagreement in a friendly and professional manner? Is there a specific reason why they might become frustrated with you? Is it possible that they will respect the way you stand by your views? That they might be able to use your arguments in their deliberations?

That they would value what you have to say? What is the worst that can happen if they become frustrated? How does it feel to disagree without telling them about it?

- What is the worst that can happen if you tell your colleague that you are worried about her? *If I tell my colleague how worried I am about her, she will break down.*

- What does 'breaking down' mean to you? Will she become psychotic, faint or start to cry? What is the worst that could happen if she started to cry? Is it possible that she might appreciate your interest and concern? That she would be relieved to get in touch with her feelings? How does it feel to be worried about her without telling her?

- What is the worst that can happen when you confront the child's parents with your suspicions about negligence? *If I confront the parents with my suspicions about child negligence, they will mistrust me and the child will be treated even worse.*

How might you confront the parents with this negligence? Can you get some help to approach this more appropriately? In which particular ways do you fear that the child will be mistreated? What is the worst that can happen if the parents mistrust you? How will it feel to do nothing?

Caring for Yourself while Caring for Others

- What is the worst that can happen if you talk to the employee about the tasks that she is not performing well enough? *If I talk to this employee about the tasks she is struggling with, she might get upset and feel criticized.*

- Is she not allowed to get upset? Is it possible for you to tell her about the tasks she has not performed well enough, without making it sound like a personal criticism? Is it possible that she will be grateful - although maybe not immediately - for the chance to improve her performance? What is the worst that can happen if you criticize her? How does it feel not to say anything to her?

- What is the worst that can happen if you say no to more night shifts? *If I say not to more night shifts I risk losing my job.*

- What is the probability of you actually losing your job if you refuse to do an extra night shift on this occasion? Is it possible that by looking after yourself in this way, you will feel less ill and more able to do your work, thereby lessening the risk of losing your job? What is the worst that can happen if you lose your job? How does it feel to say yes when, inside, you are shouting no?

- What is the worst that can happen if you tell the employee that you have doubts about her ability to do her *job? If I tell the employee that I have doubts about her ability, it will become clear that she really cannot do her job well enough.*

- What is the worst that can happen when it becomes clear to both of you that she cannot manage? Is it possible that you would both feel a lot happier if she found a job she could manage, and you were able to employ someone more suitable? How does it feel not to be aware of this?

When we give voice to our worst fears, we will often realize how unlikely it is that they will become reality. If we are in any doubt, we could consider some additional questions, as in the examples above: what is the worst that can happen if my initial fears really do become reality? Is it possible that the situation might improve if I follow my impulse? What does it feel like not to do that?

Sometimes we need to realize that following our instincts can be risky. In this way, we have identified a concrete dilemma; this is easier to relate to than a diffuse phantasy.

There is an old saying: Speak the name of the troll and he will lose his power.

I often find myself laughing when I ask the question, "What is the worst that can happen?" It feels good to realize that things are not so bad after all - and that they are not nearly as bad as I thought. And it is funny to realize how comical my fearful phantasies were.

Still, the fear of more or less realistic consequences is still present in my memory, surfacing in brief glimpses sometimes. In such cases, there are often deeper fears at play. For example when I become fearful about what others might think of my work: What if they don't think it is good enough? Underneath this thought is a deeper fear: Will I not be given any more tasks? Will I not be earning enough money? Will I not be of use?

The fear of being fired or losing one's job is quite common. This is not surprising because, deep down, this is a question of life or death. In other words, for most of us work is identified with our ability to provide for ourselves and our family, and also with the ability to be good at something, contribute to society, and to be good enough - worth enough - to exist. These are deeply existential questions. Will I be able to feed my family? Am I good enough to be allowed to exist?

In our everyday lives, we are not faced with these existential questions every time we are afraid to act on an impulse. Our fear of death will not need to be reactivated every time if we get used to asking the question, "What is the worst that can happen?" in any given situation.

Once we have become used to asking like this, we will discover that we become less fearful. We will become better at expressing ourselves more clearly. We will find it easier to ask for what we want without having to endure such unrealistic fears - and without working so hard to fight them off. In time, it will become unnecessary to ask so often, "What is the worst that can happen?"

Sometimes the answer will indicate that there is a real risk that someone will think we are weak, that they might exclude us or become frustrated with us. Or that someone will start to cry, lose faith in us or that we will hit a 'sore point'. We might risk arousing (not causing) anger and resentment. We might risk being misunderstood or ignored. And sometimes we really do risk getting fired, or not getting hired, or having to fire someone ourselves.

If that is the case - regardless of whether the consequences we fear are major or minor - we are able to think the matter through one more time, become more aware of our thought s and feelings, and then choose our course of action.

Either: "I am not prepared to expose myself or others to this right now. I would rather wait and accept that I am faced with a dilemma."

Or: "I will take this risk right now as the situation is worse than my worst fears."

You cannot know beforehand what consequences your choice will have, but you can at least choose consciously and with integrity. In this way, you are able to care for yourself and show respect for others in any given situation.

Afterthought

This little book is coming to an end. If the various questions have aroused your interest, you may want to explore them further.

Developing your ability to care for yourself is a long process. Sometimes it is all going smoothly, and then we take a step back. Perhaps you could have the book nearby, so that you can refer to it in relevant situations. You may well discover that some of the questions do not need further exploration, whereas it might feel important to keep considering others. The answers may differ from last time you explored a particular question.

In *Caring for Yourself While Caring for Others*, I chose to explore the issue of self-care from nine different angles which I consider to be relevant to many carers and caregivers. However, the issue can be explored from even more angles. At this stage, I am thinking of even more questions about your self-care.

How do you recharge when you have given so much of yourself at work? What do you give yourself? How can others be allowed to please you?

What do you choose to eat? How do you move? What entertains and inspires you?

How are you on your days off? Many helpers continue to make themselves available to others round the clock, forgetting to care for themselves at home.

How often do you do something for others - at work or in your spare time - which they could actually do themselves? Are there professional reasons when you do this? Are there other reasons such as wanting to, having surplus energy or responding with love? Are there other reasons?

How is your health? Do you sometimes go to work when you are ill? Are you familiar with ignoring your body's signals, so that you become ill?

I do not know what is healthy or true for you. You do.

Thank you for reading this.

Thank You

Thanks to Liselotte Michelsen, writing consultant, who read the first draft for this book in March 2010, commenting, "You are capable of writing a book." Since then, I have received feedback on my book from Liselotte and she has given me advice about becoming a writer.

Thanks to Kirsten Elb Jørgensen, support teacher; Susanne Stubager, care home assistant and social worker; Jette Poulsen, social worker; and to Helle Winding, senior nurse, for valuable feedback which made it clear to me that this book is important and of interest to many.

Thanks to social worker and family therapist Jette Knudsen for detailed feedback on the text. Thank you to

Anne Zimmer, who with an MA in communication proved a useful sparring partner.

Thanks to Hanne Steffensen, teacher, for her engagement and feedback on the text from the beginning - this has had a great influence on the clarity and readability of the text.

Thanks to my editor, Birgitte Lie Suhr-Jessen for receiving my manuscript with such pleasure and for her interest in the wider themes of the book.

Thanks to the hundreds of professional caregivers I have been in contact with. Colleagues, managers, employees, teachers, therapists, supervisors, sparring partners and supervisees. Your inspiration over the years has helped me write this book.

Thanks to family and friends for their support. In particular to my sister, Agnete Exner, for her support and interest - even when only being allowed to read the script at the end. And thank you to Niels Olaf Nielsen for contributing so wonderfully to a lovely atmosphere at home, providing me with excellent working conditions.

Thanks to Louise Pearlmutter, the graphic designer.